Rural Communities

by Christina Riska

Table of Contents

I need to know these words.

farmer

house

meat

motorbike

ranch

village

3

What Is a Rural Community?

Have you seen a farm? You see farms in rural communities. A rural community is outside a town or city.

▲ This boy lives in Argentina. This farm is in Argentina.

A village is a group of houses. You can see villages in rural communities.

▲ These children live in Thailand. This village is in Thailand.

Argentina is a country in South America. Argentina has rural communities.

Argentina

Thailand is a country in Asia.
Thailand has rural communities, too.

Thailand

What Work Do People Do?

Some people in Thailand are farmers.
Some farmers grow rice.

▲ This farmer grows rice in fields.

Some people in Argentina are ranchers.
Some ranchers raise animals.

▲ These ranchers ride horses.

Where Do People Live?

Look at this house. This house is in Thailand. The house has stilts. The water goes under the house.

stilts

▲ This house is in a village.

Look at these houses in Argentina. These houses are on a ranch. A ranch has grassy land for animals.

▲ This ranch is in Argentina.

What Do People Eat?

Many people eat rice in Thailand. People eat rice at most meals. The rice comes from farms.

▲ These people are eating rice.

Many people eat meat in Argentina.
The meat comes from animals.
The animals are on ranches.

▲ This man is cooking meat.

How Do People Travel?

Many people ride bicycles in Thailand. Some people ride motorbikes, too.

▲ These people are in Thailand.

Few people ride bicycles in Argentina. Some people drive cars in Argentina. Some people drive trucks.

▲ This truck belongs to a rancher.

You can compare Thailand and Argentina
How are these rural communities alike?
How are these people alike?

I Like
to Eat . . .

By John Lockyer

The monkey said,
"I **like** to eat bananas."

The pelican said,
"I **like** to eat fish."

The hippopotamus said,
"I **like** to eat grass."

4

The giraffe said,
"I **like** to eat leaves."

The mouse said,
"I **like** to eat cheese."

The frog said,
"I **like** to eat flies."

The crocodile said,
"I **like** to eat anything.
Argggh!"